THE BIG BITE
BITE
BOOK OF
Salads

THE BIG BITE BOOK OF

BOOK OF

Salads

MEG JANSZ

a Salamander book
Published by Salamander Books Limited
LONDON

A SALAMANDER BOOK

Published by Salamander Books Ltd,
129-137 York Way
London N7 9LG
United Kingdom

© Salamander Books Ltd, 1995

ISBN 0 86101 788 9

1 2 3 4 5 6 7 8 9 10

All correspondence concerning the content of this volume should be addressed to Salamander Books Ltd.

CREDITS
Author and home economist: Meg Jansz
Managing editor: Lisa Dyer
Photographer: Ken Field
Designer: Paul Johnson
Stylist: Marian Price
Filmset: SX Composing Ltd, England
Colour Separation: P&W Graphics Pte, Ltd, Singapore

Printed in Singapore

When making any of the recipes in this book, you should follow either the metric or Imperial measures, as these are not interchangeable.

Other titles of interest:
The Big Bite Book of BARBECUES
The Big Bite Book of BURGERS
The Big Bite Book of PIZZAS

CONTENTS

INTRODUCTION

The Big Bite Book of Salads contains five chapters of varied salad recipes to suit all tastes and occasions. Along with substantial main-course salads, lighter salads for eating as starters or on the side are also included, as well as a selection of fruit salads to round off a meal. All the serving sizes recommended in the recipes are for side salads, starters or light lunches, unless otherwise indicated as main-course meals. Some of the recipes are adaptations of traditional salads, while others are innovative and totally original creations.

Every civilization has eaten some mixture of raw indigenous vegetables as a health-giving part of its diet. Salads were originally the edible parts of various herbs and plants seasoned only with salt – the Latin word 'sāl', from which the word 'salad' derives.

As time progressed, the composition of salads became more varied. As early as 1699 in England, John Evelyn's *Acetaria* described 'Sallets' as 'a composition of Edule Plants and Roots of several kinds, to be eaten raw or green, blanched or candied, simple and serfe, or intermingled with others according to the season'. Evelyn recommended that the ingredients of a salad be carefully selected to complement and balance each other.

Acetaria distinguishes between simple and combined salads, however it is in classic French cooking where this distinction has evolved fully. French salads are traditionally of two types: a simple salad of tossed lettuce or another single vegetable, usually served after the main course, and a more complex combination salad, served as a separate hors d'oeuvre or even a light main course in itself.

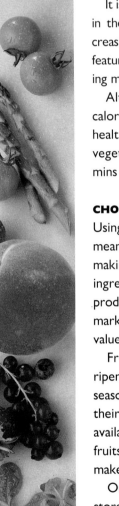

It is the combination salad that has developed in the United States of America into the increasingly popular main-course salad, which now features extremely diverse ingredients, including meat, seafood, cheese, nuts and grains.

Although many salads contain these rather calorific ingredients, salads are fundamentally healthy because their basic ingredients are raw vegetables or fruits with their inherent vitamins and minerals intact.

CHOOSING AND STORING INGREDIENTS

Using raw ingredients as the basis of your dish means that good quality is essential! For salad-making, always choose the best and freshest ingredients available. Although most fresh produce is now found, at a price, on supermarket shelves year-round, for quality and value buy produce during its growing season.

Fresh young asparagus in early summer, sun-ripened strawberries a little later on and crisp seasonal lettuce will always taste better than their forced greenhouse counterparts. The availability of root vegetables, grains, dried fruits and nuts in all seasons does enable you to make tasty salads throughout the year.

Once you have bought your ingredients, store them carefully. Salad vegetables should always be kept in a cool, dark place, preferably in a refrigerator. This will keep them firm and fresh. Fresh herbs last best in the refrigerator, either sprayed with water and placed in a polythene bag or standing in bowls of water.

RIGHT: Look for the freshest ingredients for your salads: ripe fruits, crisp lettuces and herbs, and any unusual colours or varieties.

Nuts are an excellent source of fibre and add crunch to salads. However, their shelf-life is relatively short because they have a high oil content, and can turn rancid. Buy nuts in small quantities, store them in airtight containers and use them quickly.

DRESSINGS

Dressings are an integral part of any good salad. They should always work together with the tastes of the salad ingredients, without being overpowering.

In vinaigrette dressings, my personal ideal proportions are 3 parts oil to 1 part vinegar or citrus juice. However, you should experiment and alter proportions to suit your own tastes.

Many different oils are readily available. The most popular, olive oil, is used in many classic European recipes and is a monounsaturate, generally accepted as lower in cholesterol than, for example, the more exotic nut oils. For the health-conscious, use light olive oil.

The dressings in this book use traditional oils, such as olive and sunflower, as well as more unusual newcomers, such as hazelnut, walnut, chilli and sesame oils. You may like to prepare your own flavoured oils by adding some dried chillies, garlic, or herb sprigs to a bottle of oil. If you do this, allow the flavours to develop for at least two weeks.

PREPARATION

Always ensure that all vegetables are washed before using. Washed salad leaves should be dried before dressing is added. The leaves will be crisper and the dressing will coat the leaves well. The best and quickest way to dry leaves is in a salad spinner, but a clean, dry linen towel can also be used to pat leaves dry.

If using nuts, toast them in advance as this enhances their flavour. Dressings can also be made in advance and set aside for their flavours to develop and create a stronger taste. However, dressings should be added to the salad just before serving to prevent leaves from becoming soggy. An exception is with pasta, grain and rice salads, where adding the dressings to the warm, cooked base ingredient allows the ingredient to absorb the flavours without affecting the look of the salad.

PRESENTING YOUR SALAD

The visual appeal of food is a vital part of its enjoyment, so it is worth spending time on attractive presentation. Even the simplest side salad can be made decorative by careful slicing, an imaginative combination of colours and the arrangement of the ingredients on the plate. Not all salads need to be tossed; you can arrange the ingredients on the plate, then pour or drizzle the dressing over.

Garnishing your salad before serving will also enhance its visual appeal. Garnishes can vary from a single sprig of a herb to chopped herbs sprinkled over the salad, to a single extra ingredient from the salad, such as a prawn in its shell or a spring onion tassel.

Finally, cooking and eating should be fun! Enjoy preparing and eating the salads on the following pages, but do be flexible too and experiment with the almost infinite variety of beautiful and delicious ingredients available.

RIGHT: This Three-Melon Salad (see page 66) shows how simple melon balls can look stunning. Decorative shapes for fruits and vegetables can be cut using a canelle knife, zester or peeler.

ALL-AMERICAN SALADS

This chapter includes classic favourites, such as the Waldorf Salad and the Caesar Salad, the stylish salad invented in 1924 by Caesar Cardini, which is usually finished with a flourish at your table in good restaurants. Also featured are salads that reflect the ethnic diversity of America, such as German Hot Potato Salad, and the wide range of ingredients available, such as the Lobster & Avocado Salad.

CLASSIC COLESLAW

225 g (8 oz) white cabbage
175 g (6 oz) carrots
3 sticks celery
2 small shallots, peeled
45 ml (3 tbsp) snipped fresh chives

DRESSING
90 ml (6 tbsp) mayonnaise
45 ml (3 tbsp) soured cream
15 ml (1 tbsp) white wine vinegar
15 ml (1 tbsp) water
2.5 ml (½ tsp) sugar
Salt and ground black pepper

Shred the cabbage finely. Peel the carrots and grate them coarsely. Slice the celery thinly and chop the shallots very finely. Place in a large bowl and add the snipped chives.

Place the dressing ingredients in a separate bowl and whisk well to combine. Pour over the vegetables and toss to coat. Refrigerate for at least 1 hour before serving to allow flavours to develop. SERVES 6

FRUIT & NUT SLAW

100 g (4 oz) red cabbage
100 g (4 oz) white cabbage
4 spring onions
1 carrot
2 red apples
100 g (4 oz) Brazil nuts, halved
60 ml (4 tbsp) raisins
15 ml (1 tbsp) chopped fresh parsley, to garnish

DRESSING
150 ml (10 tbsp) mayonnaise
30 ml (2 tbsp) water
2.5 ml (½ tsp) sugar
30 ml (2 tbsp) lemon juice
Salt and ground black pepper

Shred the two cabbages finely. Slice the spring onions thinly, and peel and shred the carrot. Quarter and core the apples and slice them thinly. Place the prepared vegetables and fruit in a bowl with the nuts and raisins.

Place all the dressing ingredients in a bowl and whisk well to combine. Pour the dressing over the prepared ingredients in the bowl and toss well to combine. Refrigerate for 1 hour to allow flavours to develop. Serve garnished with chopped parsley. SERVES 6

TOP: Fruit & Nut Slaw
BOTTOM: Classic Coleslaw

PRAWN & COTTAGE CHEESE SALAD IN CAPSICUM CUPS

350 g (12 oz) cottage cheese
30 ml (2 tbsp) chopped fresh dill
175 g (6 oz) cooked, peeled prawns
100 g (4 oz) seedless green grapes
1 large shallot
Salt and ground black pepper
1 medium red pepper
1 medium green pepper
100 g (4 oz) crisp lettuce leaves
½ quantity Classic French Dressing (see page 74)
4 small cooked prawns in the shell and dill sprigs,
to garnish

Place the cottage cheese, dill and prawns in a mixing bowl. Wash and halve the grapes and chop the shallot finely. Add the grapes and shallot to the bowl and season the mixture well. Mix gently to combine.

Halve the peppers lengthways, keeping the stalks intact. Remove the cores and seeds and discard. Toss the washed and dried lettuce leaves in the dressing and divide between four plates. Spoon one-quarter of the cottage cheese and prawn mixture into each pepper half. Place a filled pepper on each plate with the lettuce. Garnish each serving with a whole prawn and dill sprigs and serve at once.   SERVES 4

COBB SALAD

This salad has been made with blue Brie instead of Roquefort for a unique variation on an old favourite. You may, of course, prefer to substitute Roquefort or another blue cheese for the Brie in the recipe.

4 hard-boiled eggs
225 g (8 oz) blue Brie cheese
225 g (8 oz) cooked, skinless, boneless chicken breast
12 rashers smoked streaky bacon
6 tomatoes
12 stuffed green olives
12 stoned black olives
350 g (12 oz) iceberg lettuce, shredded
Blue Cheese Dressing, made with blue Brie
(see page 76)

Shell and slice the hard-boiled eggs. Slice the blue Brie into long thin slices. Cut the chicken into thin strips.

Cook the bacon under a preheated hot grill for about 10 minutes, turning halfway through, until it is crispy. Allow to cool, then snip into bite-sized pieces.

Cut the tomatoes into quarters, remove the seeds and chop the flesh roughly. Halve the olives.

Divide the shredded lettuce between four plates. Arrange the prepared ingredients in rows on top of the lettuce. Spoon one-quarter of the dressing on to each salad and serve immediately.

SERVES 4 AS A MAIN COURSE

RIGHT: Prawn & Cottage Cheese Salad
in Capsicum Cups

CAESAR SALAD

2 large slices, day-old white bread
120 ml (8 tbsp) olive oil
2 cloves garlic, crushed
1 Cos lettuce
8 anchovy fillets
50 g (2 oz) Parmesan cheese, grated

DRESSING

1 large egg
1 clove garlic, crushed
5 ml (1 tsp) Dijon mustard
150 ml (¼ pint) extra virgin olive oil
30 ml (2 tbsp) white wine vinegar
Salt and ground black pepper

Prepare the croûtons. Remove crusts from the bread and discard. Cut the bread into small cubes. Heat half the oil and garlic in a frying pan, add half the cubed bread and fry over a medium heat for 2-3 minutes until golden. Remove with a slotted spoon and drain on absorbant kitchen paper. Repeat with the remaining oil, garlic and bread.

Wash and dry the Cos lettuce and tear into 5-cm (2-inch) pieces. Place in a large serving bowl. Drain and rinse the anchovies and snip finely. Add to the lettuce with half the Parmesan.

Make the dressing. Place the egg in a food processor with the garlic and mustard. With the motor running, pour the oil on the egg in a thin steady stream until a thick emulsion is produced. Add the vinegar, salt and pepper and blend again briefly.

To serve, pour the dressing over the salad and toss gently. Sprinkle over the remaining Parmesan and scatter over the croûtons. Serve at once. SERVES 4

Variation: Chopped crisply cooked bacon can be added to this salad for a tasty alternative.

WESTERN SALAD

2 large slices, day-old white bread
Corn oil for deep-frying
1 Cos lettuce
25 g (1 oz) rocket leaves
175 g (6 oz) blue cheese, such as Stilton, cubed
25 g (1 oz) Parmesan cheese, grated
30 ml (2 tbsp) snipped fresh chives

DRESSING

1 egg
2 cloves garlic, crushed
150 ml (¼ pint) corn oil
30 ml (2 tbsp) lemon juice
Salt and ground black pepper

Prepare the croûtons. Remove crusts from the bread and discard. Cut the bread into small cubes. Heat the oil for deep-frying. When it is hot enough (a cube of bread dropped into the oil sizzles at the surface), fry the bread in batches for about 30 seconds until golden. Remove with a slotted spoon and drain on absorbant kitchen paper.

Make the dressing. Cook the egg in boiling water for 2 minutes to lightly soft boil it. Then spoon the soft egg into a food processor and add the garlic. With the motor running, pour the oil on to the egg in a steady stream to produce a creamy dressing. Add the lemon juice and seasoning and blend again briefly.

Wash and dry the Cos lettuce and tear into bite-sized pieces. Place in a salad bowl with the washed rocket. Add the cubed blue cheese and Parmesan.

To serve, pour over the dressing and toss gently. Scatter over the croûtons and snipped chives and serve at once.   SERVES 4

TOP: Caesar Salad
BOTTOM: Western Salad

WALDORF SALAD

250 g (9 oz) fennel
30 ml (2 tbsp) lemon juice
2 red apples
100 g (4 oz) red lettuce leaves, such as oak leaf
or lollo rosso
50 g (2 oz) walnut pieces, toasted
50 g (2 oz) raisins
Fennel fronds, to garnish

DRESSING
90 ml (6 tbsp) mayonnaise
30 ml (2 tbsp) walnut oil
30 ml (2 tbsp) lemon juice
Salt and ground black pepper

Reserve the fennel fronds and slice the fennel bulb thinly. Place in a bowl with the lemon juice, tossing gently to coat. Quarter and core the apples and slice them. Add the apples to the bowl with the fennel and toss to coat with lemon juice.

Wash and dry the lettuce. Line a shallow serving dish with the leaves. Place the dressing ingredients in a bowl and whisk well to combine.

Just before serving, drain the fennel and apple and add to the bowl of dressing along with the walnuts and raisins. Toss to combine and spoon the salad on to the bed of lettuce. Garnish with the fennel fronds and serve at once. SERVES 4-6

SWEDISH SALAD

175 g (6 oz) celery
225 g (8 oz) cooked beetroot
2 Cox's apples
50 g (2 oz) walnut halves, toasted
100 g (4 oz) radicchio leaves

DRESSING
90 ml (6 tbsp) mayonnaise
30 ml (2 tbsp) lemon juice
30 ml (2 tbsp) soured cream
Salt and ground black pepper

Slice the celery thinly on the diagonal. Cut the beetroot into wedges. Peel and core the apples and slice them. Place the celery, beetroot and apple in a large bowl. Reserve a few walnuts for garnish and add the rest to the bowl.

Place the dressing ingredients in a bowl and whisk to combine. Pour the dressing over the prepared ingredients. Toss well to mix and set aside.

Wash and dry the radicchio leaves and tear them in half. Line a salad bowl with the leaves and spoon the tossed salad into the centre. Garnish with the reserved walnuts and serve at once. SERVES 4-6

TOP: Swedish Salad
BOTTOM: Waldorf Salad

FLORIDA PRAWN SALAD

20 cooked king prawns in the shell
4 pink grapefruit
450-g (1-lb) piece Galia melon
225 g (8 oz) iceberg lettuce
20 ml (4 tsp) fresh chervil leaves

DRESSING
90 ml (6 tbsp) grapeseed oil
90 ml (6 tbsp) mayonnaise
30 ml (2 tbsp) champagne vinegar
45 ml (3 tbsp) water
1 shallot, finely chopped
15 ml (1 tbsp) crushed dried pink peppercorns
Salt and ground black pepper

Peel 12 of the prawns and halve each prawn lengthways. Keep 8 prawns whole, for garnishing. Peel the grapefruit and cut in between the membranes to produce segments.

Using a melon baller, scoop balls from the melon flesh. Wash and dry the lettuce and tear the leaves into bite-sized pieces.

Place the ingredients for the dressing in a bowl and whisk together to combine.

To assemble the salads, divide the lettuce between four plates. Arrange the prepared prawns, grapefruit segments and melon balls on the plates, spoon the dressing over the four salads and scatter over the chervil leaves. Garnish each plate with 2 whole prawns and serve at once. SERVES 4 AS A MAIN COURSE

CHEF'S SALAD

30 ml (2 tbsp) vegetable oil
350 g (12 oz) raw, skinless, boneless pieces turkey breast
Salt and ground black pepper
100 g (4 oz) honey-roast or smoked ham
225 g (8 oz) Gruyère or Emmental cheese
4 small tomatoes
4 hard-boiled eggs
350 g (12 oz) iceberg lettuce
Thousand Island Dressing (see page 76)
Parsley sprigs, to garnish

Heat the oil in a heavy-based frying pan. Season the pieces of turkey breast with salt and pepper and add to the pan. Cook over a high heat for 10 minutes, turning occasionally, until the turkey is golden on the outside and cooked through. Remove and set aside to cool.

Slice the ham into long strips. Using a swivel vegetable peeler, slice the cheese very thinly. Cut the tomatoes into wedges and shell and slice the eggs. Shred the lettuce finely. When the turkey has cooled, slice it into neat pieces.

Assemble the salads. Divide the shredded lettuce between four large plates. Arrange equal amounts of turkey, ham, cheese, tomato and egg on each plate. Spoon a little dressing into the centre of each salad and garnish with parsley. Serve at once, passing extra dressing separately. SERVES 4 AS A MAIN COURSE

RIGHT: Florida Prawn Salad

SWEET POTATO SALAD

900 g (2 lb) sweet potatoes
225 g (8 oz) carrots
1 green pepper
60 ml (4 tbsp) torn coriander leaves
Salt and ground black pepper

BUTTERMILK HERB DRESSING

90 ml (6 tbsp) buttermilk
60 ml (4 tbsp) mayonnaise
15 ml (1 tbsp) finely chopped fresh coriander
15 ml (1 tbsp) snipped fresh chives
Salt and ground black pepper

Preheat the oven to 180°C (350°F, Gas mark 4). Bake the sweet potatoes for about 40 minutes until tender. Remove from the oven and set aside to cool. When cool, peel off the skin and cut flesh into large dice.

Peel the carrots and slice them thickly. Blanch in boiling, salted water for 2-3 minutes, then drain and refresh in cold water. Halve the pepper, remove the core and seeds, and dice the flesh.

Place the dressing ingredients in a bowl and mix to combine. Place the sweet potato, carrot, pepper and torn coriander in a bowl, season well and pour over the dressing. Toss gently to combine. Refrigerate the salad for 2 hours before serving to allow the flavours to develop. SERVES 4-6

GERMAN HOT POTATO SALAD

450 g (1 lb) waxy potatoes
30 ml (2 tbsp) vegetable oil
225 g (8 oz) smoked back bacon, rinds removed and diced
1 small red onion
20 ml (4 tsp) chopped fresh sage

DRESSING

90 ml (6 tbsp) mayonnaise
30 ml (2 tbsp) milk
30 ml (2 tbsp) soured cream
10 ml (2 tsp) coarse-grain mustard
Salt and ground black pepper

Place all the dressing ingredients in a bowl and mix well to combine. Set aside.

Peel the potatoes and cut into chunks. Cook the potatoes in boiling, salted water for about 8 minutes until tender. Drain and keep warm.

While the potatoes are cooking, heat the oil in a frying pan and fry the bacon for 8-9 minutes until crisp. Keep warm.

Dice the onion finely. Place the onion, hot potatoes and bacon in a mixing bowl with the sage. Pour over the dressing, toss well and serve the salad warm. SERVES 4

TOP: German Hot Potato Salad
BOTTOM: Sweet Potato Salad

CHICKEN, GRAPE & HAZELNUT SALAD

450 g (1 lb) cooked chicken breasts
225 g (8 oz) black grapes
60 ml (4 tbsp) skinless hazelnuts, toasted
Salt and ground black pepper
225 g (8 oz) watercress
Fresh tarragon leaves, to garnish

DRESSING

2 spring onions
90 ml (6 tbsp) mayonnaise
60 ml (4 tbsp) cream cheese
90 ml (6 tbsp) water
Salt and ground black pepper

Remove the skin from the cooked chicken and discard. Cut the meat into bite-sized chunks and place in a large mixing bowl.

Wash the grapes, halve them and remove the pips. Add the grapes to the chicken along with the toasted hazelnuts. Season with salt and pepper and mix gently to combine.

Prepare the dressing. Chop the spring onions finely and place in a bowl. Add the remaining dressing ingredients and mix well. Pour the creamy dressing over the chicken and toss gently to coat.

Discard the tough stalks from the watercress. Wash and dry the watercress.

To serve, arrange a bed of watercress on a platter and spoon the chicken mixture into the centre. Garnish with tarragon and serve at once.   SERVES 4

ASPARAGUS & EGG SALAD

450 g (1 lb) fresh asparagus stalks
4 hard-boiled eggs
225 g (8 oz) sliced pastrami

BUTTERMILK DRESSING

60 ml (4 tbsp) buttermilk
60 ml (4 tbsp) olive oil
30 ml (2 tbsp) white wine vinegar
10 ml (2 tsp) coarse-grain mustard
Salt and ground black pepper

Cut the tough ends off the asparagus stalks and, using a potato peeler, peel the green skin from the asparagus stalks, stopping just below the tips. Blanch the asparagus in boiling, salted water for 2-3 minutes until just cooked. Drain and refresh in cold water.

Shell the eggs and slice each egg into 4-6 wedges. Place the ingredients for the Buttermilk Dressing in a bowl and whisk to combine.

To serve, arrange the asparagus, egg wedges and sliced pastrami on four serving plates. Drizzle some dressing over each portion and serve at once.

SERVES 4

RIGHT: Chicken, Grape & Hazelnut Salad

LOBSTER & AVOCADO SALAD

2 small boiled lobsters
8 asparagus stalks, preferably white
1 large, ripe avocado
20 ml (4 tsp) lemon juice
100 g (4 oz) mixed lettuce leaves
Tarragon sprigs, to garnish

DRESSING

30 ml (2 tbsp) olive oil
60 ml (4 tbsp) sunflower oil
30 ml (2 tbsp) tarragon vinegar
10 ml (2 tsp) finely chopped shallot
20 ml (4 tsp) chopped fresh tarragon
10 ml (2 tsp) Dijon mustard
5 ml (1 tsp) sugar
Salt and ground black pepper

Prepare the lobsters. Twist off the claws and crack them. Either leave the claws ready for eating or remove the flesh. For each lobster, gently separate the tail from the head and body. With sharp scissors cut down the length of the underside of the tail. Bend apart so the meat becomes free and remove the vein. Remove the flesh and slice into thick discs.

Cut the tough ends from the asparagus and slice each stalk in half lengthways. Blanch in boiling, salted water for 2 minutes. Drain and refresh under cold water. Peel the avocado, halve and slice the flesh thickly; then place in a bowl with the lemon juice.

Wash and dry the lettuce. Place the dressing ingredients in a bowl and whisk to combine.

To assemble, toss the lettuce with half the dressing and divide between two plates. Arrange the lobster, asparagus and avocado on each bed of lettuce. Spoon the remaining dressing over the salads, garnish with tarragon and serve at once.

SERVES 2 AS A MAIN COURSE

CRAB LOUIS SALAD

350 g (12 oz) fresh crabmeat
1 onion
100 g (4 oz) celery
12 stuffed olives
Salt and ground black pepper
Pinch of cayenne
100 g (4 oz) iceberg lettuce
Celery leaves, to garnish

DRESSING

60 ml (4 tbsp) mayonnaise
60 ml (4 tbsp) cream, very lightly whipped
60 ml (4 tbsp) chilli sauce
1 small green chilli, seeded and chopped
60 ml (4 tbsp) fresh chervil leaves
Salt and ground black pepper

Place all the dressing ingredients in a bowl and mix well to combine. Refrigerate while preparing the salad to allow the flavours to develop.

Flake the crabmeat and place in a mixing bowl. Peel the onion and grate coarsely. Wash the celery and slice thinly on the diagonal. Halve the olives. Add the ingredients to the crabmeat and season with salt, pepper and cayenne. Add the dressing and toss well.

Wash and dry the lettuce. Divide the lettuce between four plates and spoon one-quarter of the crab salad on to each plate. Garnish with celery leaves and serve at once. SERVES 4

TOP: Crab Louis Salad
BOTTOM: Lobster & Avocado Salad

WILD RICE SALAD WITH SCALLOPS

225 g (8 oz) mixed long-grain and wild rice
2 spring onions
2 large carrots
½ red pepper
½ orange pepper
30 ml (2 tbsp) pumpkin seeds
450 g (1 lb) large scallops with corals
45 ml (3 tbsp) vegetable oil

DRESSING

Grated zest of 1 lime
60 ml (4 tbsp) lime juice
90 ml (6 tbsp) sunflower oil
1 large clove garlic, crushed
20 ml (4 tsp) chopped fresh flat-leaved parsley
Pinch of sugar
Salt and ground black pepper

Cook the rice in boiling, salted water according to the instructions on the packet. Drain and refresh in cold water. Set aside.

Slice the spring onions into long, thin strips. Peel the carrots and, using a vegetable peeler, peel the carrots into long ribbons. Blanch the carrot ribbons in boiling, salted water for about 1 minute. Drain and refresh in cold water.

Remove the cores from the peppers and dice the flesh finely. Toast the pumpkin seeds under a hot grill for 2 minutes until pale golden. Remove the seeds and allow to cool.

Separate the scallop corals from the whites. Cut each scallop white into quarters and halve the corals. Heat half the oil in a frying pan and sauté the whites, stirring frequently, for about 3 minutes. Remove the scallops from the pan. Add the remaining oil to the pan and sauté the corals for 3 minutes. Remove the corals from the pan.

Place the ingredients for the dressing in a screw-topped jar and shake well to mix. Pour half the dressing over the rice and toss gently to coat. Place the rice in a serving dish.

Mix together the remaining ingredients, except the pumpkin seeds, and pour over the remaining dressing. Toss gently and spoon over the rice. Scatter over the pumpkin seeds and serve at once. SERVES 4-6

BLACK-EYED SUSAN SALAD

4 grapefruit
4 dates
40 g (1½ oz) pecan nuts
175 g (6 oz) mixed lettuce leaves, to include rocket, Cos and lamb's lettuce
Classic French Dressing (see page 74)

Using a sharp knife, peel the skin and white pith from the grapefruit and cut between the membranes to produce segments.

Remove the stones from the dates and slice the flesh into long segments. Cut the pecan nuts lengthways into quarters. Wash and dry the lettuce and tear large leaves into bite-sized pieces.

To serve, toss the lettuce with half the dressing and divide between four plates. Arrange the grapefruit in a spoke-like pattern over the lettuce and arrange the dates and pecan nuts in the centre. Spoon the remaining dressing over the salads and serve at once.

SERVES 4

TOP: Wild Rice Salad with Scallops
BOTTOM: Black-eyed Susan Salad

EUROPEAN SALADS

The surprisingly diverse flavours and ingredients of this small continent feature in the recipes in this chapter. Along with Caponata from Sicily, with its colourful variety of vegetables, and the French Salade Niçoise, with its Mediterranean taste, are the German Kartoffelsalat and the Norwegian Herring & Dill Salad, with their subtler, northern flavours.

GREEK SALAD

350 g (12 oz) feta cheese
4 plum tomatoes
½ cucumber
1 small purple onion
16 oil-cured Greek olives
Oregano sprigs, to garnish

HERB DRESSING
90 ml (6 tbsp) extra virgin olive oil, preferably Greek
30 ml (2 tbsp) white wine vinegar
45 ml (3 tbsp) chopped fresh oregano
1 large clove garlic, crushed
Pinch of sugar
Salt and ground black pepper

Place all the dressing ingredients in a screw-topped jar and shake well to combine. Chill until required.

Cube the feta cheese and cut the tomatoes into wedges. Place in a large salad bowl.

Halve the cucumber and dice. Peel and thinly slice the onion. Add the cucumber and onion to the salad with the olives. Pour over the dressing and toss well. Serve at once.　　　　　SERVES 4

TOMATO SALAD WITH HALLOUMI & ROCKET

8 small, ripe plum tomatoes
100 g (4 oz) halloumi cheese
2 spring onions
150 g (5 oz) rocket leaves
12 black olives

DRESSING
90 ml (6 tbsp) extra virgin olive oil
30 ml (2 tbsp) red wine vinegar
30 ml (2 tbsp) chopped fresh oregano
Salt and ground black pepper
Pinch of sugar

Wash the tomatoes and slice thickly. Cut the halloumi cheese into thin strips. Shred the spring onions into long, thin strips.

Wash and dry the rocket and tear any large leaves into bite-sized pieces; then line a serving plate with the leaves. Arrange the tomatoes and cheese on the bed of rocket and scatter over the spring onions and olives.

Place the dressing ingredients in a screw-topped jar and shake well to combine. Spoon the dressing over the prepared salad and serve at once.　　SERVES 4-6

TOP: Greek Salad
BOTTOM: Tomato Salad
with Halloumi & Rocket

FRENCH FRISEE SALAD WITH GARLIC CROUTONS

175 g (6 oz) frisée lettuce

GARLIC CROUTONS

4 cloves garlic, crushed
90 ml (6 tbsp) extra virgin olive oil
Salt and ground black pepper
75 g (3 oz) crustless white bread

ROQUEFORT DRESSING

45 ml (3 tbsp) corn oil
45 ml (3 tbsp) mayonnaise
30 ml (2 tbsp) white wine vinegar
30 ml (2 tbsp) water
2.5 ml (½ tsp) Dijon mustard
Few drops Worcestershire sauce
Salt and ground black pepper
100 g (4 oz) Roquefort cheese

Prepare the croûtons. Preheat the oven to 180°C (350°F, Gas mark 4). Place the garlic, oil and seasoning in a large bowl and mix well. Cut the bread into 1.5-cm (½-inch) cubes and add to the bowl. Toss well to coat. Transfer the bread to a baking sheet and bake on the top shelf of the oven for about 15 minutes until golden. Remove and set aside.

Place all the dressing ingredients, except the cheese, in a bowl and whisk to combine. Mash the cheese with a fork and add it, a little at a time, to the dressing, whisking well between each addition.

Wash and dry the frisée lettuce and tear into bite-sized pieces. Place in a bowl with half the croûtons, pour over the dressing and toss until evenly coated with dressing. Serve the salad at once with the remaining croûtons scattered over the top.   SERVES 4

SALADE NICOISE

198-g (7-oz) can tuna in oil, drained and flaked
100 g (4 oz) fine French beans
100 g (4 oz) baby broad beans
6 anchovy fillets
½ cucumber
4 tomatoes
20 black olives
3 hard-boiled eggs, shelled
Chicory leaves, to serve

DRESSING

90 ml (6 tbsp) French olive oil
30 ml (2 tbsp) white wine vinegar
1 clove garlic, crushed
5 ml (1 tsp) Dijon mustard
45 ml (3 tbsp) chopped flat-leaved parsley
Salt and ground black pepper

Place the dressing ingredients in a screw-topped jar and shake well to combine. Set aside.

Place the flaked tuna in a mixing bowl. Halve the French beans and blanch them in boiling, salted water with the broad beans for 3 minutes until just tender. Drain and refresh in cold water.

Cut the anchovy fillets into small pieces and slice the cucumber into batons. Cut the tomatoes into wedges. Add beans, anchovy, cucumber and tomato to the tuna along with the olives. Pour over the dressing and toss the salad gently.

Wash and dry the chicory and line a serving dish with the leaves. Spoon the prepared salad into the centre. Cut each egg into quarters and add to the salad. Serve at once.   SERVES 4

TOP: French Frisée Salad
BOTTOM: Salade Niçoise

WARM CHICKEN LIVER, SUN-DRIED TOMATO & PASTA SALAD

225 g (8 oz) dried pasta shapes
60 ml (4 tbsp) olive oil
3 shallots, sliced
2 cloves garlic, crushed
450 g (1 lb) chicken livers, trimmed
Salt and ground black pepper
8 halves sun-dried tomatoes in oil, drained and sliced
100 g (4 oz) frisée lettuce, washed and torn into bite-sized pieces

DRESSING

60 ml (4 tbsp) oil from sun-dried tomatoes
60 ml (4 tbsp) olive oil
60 ml (4 tbsp) balsamic vinegar
60 ml (4 tbsp) chopped fresh parsley
10 ml (2 tsp) Dijon mustard
Salt and ground black pepper

Place all the dressing ingredients in a screw-topped jar and shake well.

Cook the pasta in plenty of boiling, salted water for about 10 minutes or until 'al dente'. Drain the pasta and immediately toss it with the prepared dressing while still warm. Set aside.

Heat the oil in a large frying pan and sauté the shallots and garlic for 1 minute until softened. Add the chicken livers, season well and sauté for a further 4-5 minutes until browned on the outside and just cooked in the centre. Transfer the chicken livers to the bowl of pasta. Add the sun-dried tomatoes and toss well to combine. Serve the warm salad immediately, on a bed of frisée lettuce.   SERVES 6

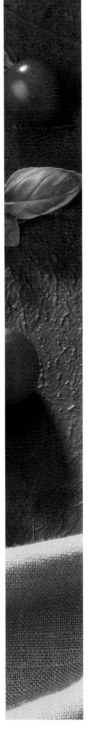

SMOKED DUCK & PESTO PASTA SALAD

100 g (4 oz) dried pasta shapes
175 g (6 oz) cooked, smoked duck breast
12 cherry tomatoes
60 ml (4 tbsp) pine nuts, toasted
175 g (6 oz) mixed salad leaves
Basil sprigs, to garnish

PESTO DRESSING

60 ml (4 tbsp) pesto sauce
90 ml (6 tbsp) vegetable oil
30 ml (2 tbsp) red wine vinegar
Salt and ground black pepper

Place all the dressing ingredients in a bowl and whisk to combine.

Cook the pasta in plenty of boiling, salted water for 8-10 minutes or until 'al dente'. Drain the pasta and immediately toss it with the prepared dressing. Set aside.

Slice the duck into thin strips and halve the cherry tomatoes. Add to the bowl of pasta along with the pine nuts. Toss well.

Wash the lettuce leaves and tear large leaves in half. Line a serving bowl with the lettuce and spoon the pasta salad into the centre. Garnish with basil and serve at once.   SERVES 4

RIGHT: Smoked Duck & Pesto Pasta Salad

AVOCADO, MOZZARELLA & BAKED TOMATO SALAD

The baked tomatoes in this salad take a long time to cook and, for convenience, can be prepared the day before and stored in an airtight container in the refrigerator until required.

150 g (5 oz) mini mozzarella cheeses
2 ripe avocados
15 ml (1 tbsp) lemon juice
Basil leaves, to garnish

BAKED TOMATOES

6 small, ripe plum tomatoes
Olive oil to drizzle
A little caster sugar
Sea salt and ground black pepper

DRESSING

120 ml (8 tbsp) extra virgin olive oil
30 ml (2 tbsp) balsamic vinegar
60 ml (4 tbsp) torn basil leaves
Salt and ground black pepper

Prepare the baked tomatoes. Preheat the oven to 100°C (200°F, Gas mark ¼). Blanch the tomatoes for 20 seconds in boiling, salted water to loosen their skins. When cooled, peel off the skin, halve, and scoop out the seeds. Place cut-side down on a greased baking sheet. Drizzle each tomato with a little olive oil and sprinkle with a little sugar, salt and pepper. Bake for 1 hour. Turn over, drizzle with a little more oil and bake for a further hour. Remove and allow to cool.

Slice the mini mozzarella into thick slices. Peel and stone the avocados and slice the flesh. Sprinkle the avocados with lemon juice.

Mix together the dressing ingredients. To serve, arrange the tomatoes, cheese and avocado on four plates. Spoon dressing over each salad, garnish with basil and serve at once. SERVES 4

ROCKET, BACON & AVOCADO SALAD

12 rashers rindless, streaky bacon
2 small avocados
15 ml (1 tbsp) lemon juice
175 g (6 oz) rocket leaves
90 ml (6 tbsp) finely grated Parmesan cheese
Ground black pepper
Italian Balsamic Dressing (see page 74)

Place the bacon rashers under a preheated hot grill and grill for about 8 minutes, turning halfway through cooking, until crisp and golden. Remove and drain on absorbent kitchen paper. When cool, snip the bacon into bite-sized pieces with kitchen scissors.

Peel and stone the avocado and cut the flesh into chunks. Place in a bowl with the lemon juice. Wash and dry the rocket leaves and place in a salad bowl. Add the bacon, avocado and 60 ml (4 tbsp) of the Parmesan. Add some black pepper and pour over the prepared dressing. Toss the salad gently and serve with the remaining Parmesan sprinkled over the top. SERVES 4

TOP: Avocado, Mozzarella
& Baked Tomato Salad
BOTTOM: Rocket, Bacon & Avocado Salad

CAPONATA

This salad is best made a day in advance and stored in the refrigerator to allow the flavours to develop.

90 ml (6 tbsp) extra virgin olive oil
1 red onion, sliced into rings
2 cloves garlic, sliced into slivers
1 large aubergine
2 ripe beef tomatoes
2 courgettes
2 yellow peppers
30 ml (2 tbsp) sun-dried tomato paste
Salt and ground black pepper
30 ml (2 tbsp) red wine vinegar
30 ml (2 tbsp) chopped fresh flat-leaved parsley
15 ml (1 tbsp) chopped fresh thyme
16 small black olives
8 anchovy fillets
2 Little Gem lettuces, washed and separated into leaves
Flat-leaved parsley sprig, to garnish

Preheat the oven to 180°C (350°F, Gas mark 4). Heat half the oil in a large, heavy-based, ovenproof saucepan. Add the onion and sauté for 2 minutes. Stir in the garlic and sauté for a further minute. Set aside.

Cut the aubergine into 1.5-cm (½-inch) cubes. Peel and seed the tomatoes and cut into large dice. Slice the courgettes. Cut the peppers into 1.5-cm (½-inch) cubes. Add the vegetables to the pan.

Stir the sun-dried tomato paste into the pan and season the vegetables well. Cook over a low heat for 5 minutes, then cover the pan and transfer to the oven. Bake for 40 minutes.

Place the remaining olive oil in a screw-topped jar with the vinegar, parsley, thyme and seasoning. Shake well to combine. Cut each anchovy fillet into four.

Stir the dressing, anchovies and olives into the warm vegetables. Allow to cool.

Just before serving, line a dish with the lettuce leaves. Using a slotted spoon, spoon the caponata on to the lettuce. Serve garnished with parsley sprigs.
SERVES 4

ORANGE & PURPLE ONION SALAD

6 large oranges
1 large purple onion
12 black olives (optional)

POPPYSEED DRESSING
90 ml (6 tbsp) extra virgin olive oil
30 ml (2 tbsp) fresh orange juice
15 ml (1 tbsp) white wine vinegar
7.5 ml (1½ tsp) clear honey
10 ml (2 tsp) poppyseeds
Salt and ground black pepper

Peel the oranges using a small sharp knife, taking care to remove all the white pith. Slice the oranges thickly and arrange them in overlapping circles on a shallow serving plate.

Slice the purple onion into thin rings. Arrange the onion on top of the oranges and scatter over the black olives, if desired.

Place the dressing ingredients in a screw-topped jar and shake well to combine. Spoon the dressing over the salad and serve at once. SERVES 4-6

TOP: Caponata
BOTTOM: Orange & Purple Onion Salad

GREEN LENTIL SALAD

175 g (6 oz) Puy lentils, soaked for 1 hour
1 orange pepper
1 red pepper
3 spring onions
100 g (4 oz) Escarole lettuce leaves
Oregano sprigs, to garnish

DRESSING

60 ml (4 tbsp) yoghurt
30 ml (2 tbsp) olive oil
45 ml (3 tbsp) chopped fresh parsley
45 ml (3 tbsp) chopped fresh oregano
1 large clove garlic, crushed
1.25 ml (¼ tsp) paprika
Salt and ground black pepper

Place all the dressing ingredients in a bowl and whisk to combine. Set aside.

Drain the soaked lentils and place in a saucepan of fresh water with a little salt. Boil the lentils gently for about 20 minutes or until tender, then drain. While still warm, toss the lentils with the dressing to allow the flavours to absorb. Set aside.

Halve the peppers and remove the cores and seeds. Grill under a preheated hot grill for about 10 minutes until the skins are charred. Remove and cover the peppers with damp absorbent kitchen paper to make them easier to peel. Once cool, peel off the skins and slice the flesh into thin strips. Chop the spring onions finely and add to the lentils along with the peppers. Toss well. Wash and dry the lettuce leaves and serve the salad on a bed of Escarole lettuce, garnished with oregano sprigs. SERVES 6

TURKISH SALAD

Labna balls are strained yoghurt balls preserved in oil. Herbs are sometimes added to the oil. They are available in jars from good continental delicatessens.

2 courgettes
½ onion
8 labna balls in oil, drained
6 artichoke hearts in oil, drained
1 Cos lettuce
60 ml (4 tbsp) finely diced red pepper

DRESSING

30 ml (2 tbsp) oil from the jar of labna balls
30 ml (2 tbsp) extra virgin olive oil
30 ml (2 tbsp) lemon juice
2.5 ml (½ tsp) ground cumin
1.25 ml (¼ tsp) chilli powder
Salt and ground black pepper
Pinch of sugar

Place all the dressing ingredients in a small saucepan. Whisk to combine and heat the dressing very gently to warm it.

Using a vegetable peeler, peel long ribbons of courgette. Slice the onion very thinly. Place the courgette ribbons and sliced onions in a bowl, pour over the warm dressing and toss gently to combine. Set aside.

Halve the labna balls and the artichokes. Wash and dry the lettuce and tear the leaves into bite-sized pieces. Divide the lettuce between four plates. Add the labna balls and artichoke hearts to the courgettes and onions, and toss gently to coat with the dressing. Divide the mixture between the plates. Sprinkle one-quarter of the diced red pepper over each salad and serve at once. SERVES 4

RIGHT: Turkish Salad

GREEK PEACH & GRILLED GREEN PEPPER SALAD

4 green peppers
2 large, ripe peaches
175 g (6 oz) feta cheese
12 calamata olives

CUMIN DRESSING

10 ml (2 tsp) cumin seeds
120 ml (8 tbsp) olive oil
45 ml (3 tbsp) white wine vinegar
Salt and ground black pepper
Pinch of sugar

Halve the peppers lengthways and remove the cores and seeds. Place them cut-side down on a baking sheet and grill under a preheated hot grill for 8-10 minutes or until the skins are charred. Remove and cover the peppers with damp absorbant kitchen paper to make them easier to peel. Once cool, peel off the charred skins and slice the flesh into thick strips.

Halve and stone the peaches and slice the flesh thickly. Cut the feta into small cubes. Place the peppers, peaches, feta and olives in a mixing bowl.

Make the dressing. Dry-roast the cumin seeds in a frying pan for about I minute, until they begin to pop and their aroma is released. Transfer to a bowl with the remaining dressing ingredients and mix well.

Pour the dressing over the salad ingredients and toss gently. Refrigerate for I hour before serving.

SERVES 4

SPICED RICE SALAD

100 g (4 oz) brown long-grain rice
100 g (4 oz) white long-grain rice
50 g (2 oz) fresh dates
75 g (3 oz) dried apricots
50 g (2 oz) shelled pistachio nuts
60 ml (4 tbsp) snipped fresh chives
Coriander sprigs, to garnish

DRESSING

75 ml (5 tbsp) pistachio or corn oil
45 ml (3 tbsp) lime juice
45 ml (3 tbsp) chopped fresh coriander
2.5 ml (½ tsp) chilli powder
Salt and ground black pepper

Place all the dressing ingredients in a screw-topped jar and shake well to combine.

Cook the two types of rice in separate saucepans of boiling, salted water, following the cooking instructions on the packets. Once cooked, drain and mix the warm rice with the dressing. The rice will absorb the flavour of the dressing. Set aside.

Remove the stones from the dates and cut the flesh into long slivers. Cut the apricots into quarters. Add the dates and apricots to the rice along with the pistachios and chives. Toss well. Serve the salad at room temperature, garnished with coriander sprigs.

SERVES 4

TOP: Spiced Rice Salad
BOTTOM: Greek Peach & Grilled
Green Pepper Salad

NORWEGIAN HERRING & DILL SALAD

450 g (1 lb) baby new potatoes
4 pickled herrings
2 small shallots
12 chicory leaves, preferably red
1 soft lettuce heart

DRESSING
90 ml (6 tbsp) sunflower oil
60 ml (4 tbsp) chopped fresh dill
45 ml (3 tbsp) Dijon mustard
45 ml (3 tbsp) cider vinegar
25-30 ml (1½-2 tbsp) caster sugar
Sea salt and ground black pepper

First prepare the dressing. Place the oil, dill, mustard and vinegar in a bowl. Add 25 ml (1½ tbsp) of the sugar and season generously. Whisk until well combined. Taste and add the extra sugar and more seasoning if necessary: the dressing should be thick, sweet and mustardy. Set aside.

Scrub the potatoes. Place in a saucepan of salted water, bring to the boil, then reduce heat and cook on a medium boil for about 12 minutes or until tender. Drain and refresh in cold water. When the potatoes are cool enough to handle, slice them thickly.

Slice the herrings into 2.5-cm (1-inch) pieces. Peel and thinly slice the shallots. Place the potatoes, herrings and shallots in a bowl, pour over the dressing and toss well.

Separate the lettuce heart into leaves. Wash and dry the lettuce and chicory leaves. Line a serving bowl with the leaves and spoon the salad into the centre. Serve at once.   SERVES 4

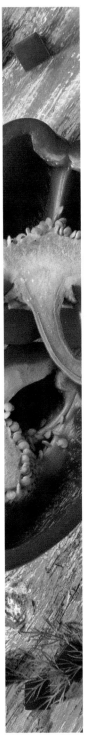

KARTOFFELSALAT

1 large red pepper
2 spring onions
450 g (1 lb) baby new potatoes
325 g (8 oz) frankfurters (about 8 small frankfurters)

MUSTARD MAYONNAISE
120 ml (8 tbsp) mayonnaise
20 ml (4 tsp) German mustard
30 ml (2 tbsp) chopped fresh dill
30 ml (2 tbsp) milk
Pinch of sugar
Salt and ground black pepper

Place all the mayonnaise ingredients in a bowl and whisk to combine. Set the mayonnaise dressing aside, but do not refrigerate it.

Halve the pepper, remove the core and seeds and dice the flesh. Slice the spring onions thinly on the diagonal. Place the prepared peppers and spring onions in a serving bowl.

Scrub the potatoes and halve them. Place them in a saucepan of salted water, bring to the boil, then reduce heat and cook on a medium boil for 10-12 minutes until tender. Drain the potatoes and add to the serving bowl.

While the potatoes are cooking, cook the frankfurters according to the instructions on the packet. Drain and slice thickly on the diagonal. Add to the serving bowl.

Pour the dressing over the warm potatoes, frankfurters and prepared peppers and spring onions. Toss to combine and serve at once while the salad is warm.
SERVES 4-6

RIGHT: Kartoffelsalat

BRITISH BEEF SALAD

550-g (1¼-lb) piece beef fillet
Ground black pepper
15 ml (1 tbsp) vegetable oil
700 g (1½ lb) baby new potatoes
225 g (8 oz) shelled baby broad beans
12 cherry tomatoes
175 g (6 oz) soft lettuce heart leaves
Horseradish Dressing (see page 78)
Curly parsley sprigs, to garnish

Preheat the oven to 110°C (225°F, Gas mark ¼). Cut the beef fillet in half and coat each piece generously with pepper. Heat the oil in a heavy-based frying pan and sear the pieces of beef over a high heat, turning so they brown all over, for 6-8 minutes. Transfer the beef to a roasting tin and bake for 1 hour and 10 minutes. This method will produce very tender, medium-rare meat. Allow beef to cool.

Scrub the potatoes and place in a saucepan of salted water. Bring to the boil, then reduce to a medium heat and simmer for 10-12 minutes until tender. Drain and refresh in cold water. Slice the cooled potatoes in half.

Cook the broad beans in boiling, salted water for about 5 minutes until tender. Drain and refresh in cold water. Halve the cherry tomatoes. Slice the cooled beef into strips and place the meat in a bowl with the potatoes, broad beans and tomatoes. Pour over the dressing and toss well.

Wash the lettuce leaves and divide the lettuce between four plates. Spoon one-quarter of the beef salad on to each plate. Garnish with parsley sprigs and serve at once.   SERVES 4 AS A MAIN COURSE

GRILLED GOAT'S CHEESE SALAD

75 g (3 oz) mixed salad leaves, to include oak leaf, baby spinach and lollo rosso
½ small ripe pear, cored and sliced
4 slices ciabatta bread
175 g (6 oz) goat's cheese
15 ml (1 tbsp) walnut oil

DRESSING
30 ml (2 tbsp) walnut oil
15 ml (1 tbsp) vegetable oil
15 ml (1 tbsp) white wine vinegar
2.5 ml (½ tsp) Dijon mustard
Pinch of sugar
Salt and ground black pepper

Place the dressing ingredients in a screw-topped jar and shake well to combine. Set aside.

Wash and dry the lettuce and tear large leaves into bite-sized pieces. Place in a bowl with the sliced pears and pour over the dressing. Toss gently to coat and divide between two plates.

Place the bread under a preheated hot grill and toast on one side until lightly golden. Remove and turn the bread over.

Slice the cheese into four pieces and place a piece of cheese on the untoasted side of each bread slice. Drizzle with walnut oil and add some black pepper. Return to the grill and grill for about 2 minutes or until cheese begins to melt. Place two slices of bread and cheese on each plate of salad and serve at once.   SERVES 2

TOP: British Beef Salad
BOTTOM: Grilled Goat's Cheese Salad

EXOTIC & ORIENTAL SALADS

The recipes in this chapter are inspired by the cuisines of South-east Asia and the Far East, as well as the Caribbean and Mexico. For a delicious and substantial main course, try Salmon Teriyaki Salad or, if you like spicy food, experience the robust flavours of Thai Beef Salad. There are also recipes for the vegetarian, such as Mexican Bean Salad and Tofu & Oriental Mushroom Salad.

MEXICAN BEAN SALAD

432-g (15-oz) can red kidney beans
432-g (15-oz) can black-eyed beans
Heart of 1 Cos lettuce
2 small avocados

LIME AND CORIANDER DRESSING
Juice of 1½ limes
Grated zest of ½ lime
90 ml (6 tbsp) sunolive or light olive oil
45 ml (3 tbsp) chopped fresh coriander
5 ml (1 tsp) crushed pink and black peppercorns
Sea salt and pinch of sugar

Place all the dressing ingredients in a screw-topped jar and shake well to combine. Chill until required.

Drain the canned beans and rinse well. Separate the Cos lettuce leaves and wash and dry them.

Line a flat bowl with the lettuce leaves. Peel, stone and slice the avocados, and mix in a large bowl with the beans and dressing. Spoon the salad on to the bed of lettuce and serve at once.   SERVES 4-6

MEXICAN FISH SALAD

225 g (8 oz) red snapper fillets
Fish stock for poaching
1 small ripe mango
1 green pepper
1 fresh red chilli
2 sticks celery
75 g (3 oz) crisp lettuce leaves
15 ml (1 tbsp) coriander leaves, to garnish

DRESSING
60 ml (4 tbsp) mayonnaise
15 ml (1 tbsp) vegetable oil
15 ml (1 tbsp) chopped fresh coriander
5 ml (1 tsp) cayenne
½ red chilli, seeded and finely chopped
Juice of 1 lime
Hot chilli sauce, to taste

Poach the snapper fillets in lightly simmering fish stock for 5-6 minutes until cooked. Remove, discard the stock and allow to cool. When cool, flake the fish.

Cut the mango flesh from the stone and slice thinly. Halve, core and seed the pepper and slice the flesh. Slice the chilli into rings. Slice the celery on the diagonal. Wash and dry the lettuce and tear the leaves into bite-sized pieces.

Place the dressing ingredients in a bowl and whisk together until combined. Set aside.

To serve, arrange the lettuce, mango, pepper, chilli and celery on two plates. Pour the dressing over the fish and toss lightly to combine. Spoon half the fish on to each bed of salad, garnish with coriander and serve at once.   SERVES 2 AS A MAIN COURSE

TOP: Mexican Bean Salad
BOTTOM: Mexican Fish Salad

CAJUN CHICKEN SALAD

4 skinless, boneless chicken breasts
25 g (1 oz) unsalted butter, melted
2 corn on the cob, each cut into 6 pieces
2 large red peppers
175 g (6 oz) iceberg lettuce, coarsely shredded
Oregano sprigs, to garnish

SEASONING MIX

7.5 ml (1½ tsp) salt
15 ml (1 tbsp) paprika
5 ml (1 tsp) dried onion granules
5 ml (1 tsp) dried garlic granules
5 ml (1 tsp) dried thyme
5 ml (1 tsp) cayenne
2.5 ml (½ tsp) cracked black pepper
2.5 ml (½ tsp) dried oregano

SPICY DRESSING

90 ml (6 tbsp) corn oil
30 ml (2 tbsp) lemon juice
1 shallot, finely chopped
1.25 ml (¼ tsp) cayenne
5 ml (1 tsp) Dijon mustard
5 ml (1 tsp) chopped fresh thyme
Pinch of sugar
Salt and ground black pepper

Place all the dressing ingredients in a screw-topped jar and shake to combine. Chill until required.

Mix together all the seasoning mix ingredients. Flatten each chicken breast with a mallet, between sheets of cling film, until about 1.5-cm (½-inch) thick. Brush each chicken breast with some melted butter and press one-quarter of the seasoning mix over each breast to coat completely. Set aside.

Cook the corn in boiling, salted water for 20-25 minutes until tender. Divide each pepper in half lengthways, core and seed, and brush with a little olive

oil. Grill the peppers for 10-15 minutes, turning occasionally until slightly charred. Keep warm.

Heat a heavy cast-iron frying pan over a high heat until the pan is smoking and very hot. Add the chicken and cook for 8-10 minutes, turning occasionally, until the outside is blackened and chicken is cooked.

Toss the iceberg lettuce in the dressing. Cut the red pepper into thick strips. Divide the lettuce between four plates. Slice the chicken breasts and divide between the plates. Place three pieces of corn and some red pepper strips on each plate. Serve at once.

SERVES 4 AS A MAIN COURSE

TABBOULEH

225 g (8 oz) bulghur wheat
50 g (2 oz) flat-leaved parsley, finely chopped
25 g (1 oz) mint leaves, finely chopped
6 spring onions, sliced
2 beef tomatoes, skinned, seeded and chopped
100 g (4 oz) cucumber, very finely chopped

DRESSING

3 cloves garlic, crushed
Juice of 2 lemons
90 ml (6 tbsp) extra virgin olive oil
Salt and ground black pepper

Place the bulghur wheat in a bowl and just cover with boiling water. Set aside for 30 minutes to allow the water to absorb. Drain thoroughly, place in a clean linen towel and squeeze to remove excess moisture. Place the bulghur wheat in a large bowl and stir in the remaining ingredients.

Place the dressing ingredients in a screw-topped jar and shake well to combine. Pour over the salad, toss gently and set aside for 30 minutes to allow the flavours to develop.
SERVES 6

RIGHT: Cajun Chicken Salad

BALINESE DUCK SALAD

2 × 225 g (8 oz) duck breasts
Groundnut oil for frying
50 g (2 oz) Cos lettuce
50 g (2 oz) Chinese pak choy
100 g (4 oz) beansprouts, washed
4 spring onions, sliced on the diagonal
75 g (3 oz) cucumber, cut into matchsticks

MARINADE
4 shallots, chopped
4 cloves garlic, chopped
4 green chillies, seeded and chopped
5-cm (2-inch) piece root ginger, peeled and chopped
2.5 ml (½ tsp) turmeric
10 ml (2 tsp) galangal powder
Salt and ground black pepper

DRESSING
15 ml (1 tbsp) groundnut oil
Juice of 1 lime
3 Kaffir lime leaves, finely chopped
1 stalk lemon grass, finely chopped
10 ml (2 tsp) clear honey
Salt and ground black pepper

Place the marinade ingredients in a blender and process to produce a smooth paste. Slash each duck breast and spread the marinade all over. Refrigerate for at least 1 hour. Place the dressing ingredients in a bowl and whisk to combine. Set aside.

Lightly oil a heavy-based frying pan and cook the duck over a high heat for about 6 minutes on each side. Remove from heat. Slice the duck diagonally.

Wash and dry the Cos and pak choy and tear the leaves into bite-sized pieces. Place in a bowl with the beansprouts, spring onions and cucumber. Pour over the dressing and toss well. Divide the salad and duck between four plates and serve at once. SERVES 4

CARIBBEAN PORK SALAD

450 g (1 lb) pork tenderloin, cut into long strips
225 g (8 oz) cubed pumpkin
30 ml (2 tbsp) vegetable oil
1 onion, sliced
1 green pepper, sliced into rings
100 g (4 oz) mixed salad leaves

SEASONING MIXTURE
10 ml (2 tsp) allspice berries, crushed
2 hot Jamaican peppers, seeded and finely chopped
10 ml (2 tsp) chopped fresh thyme
10 ml (2 tsp) cayenne
2 spring onions, finely chopped
2 cloves garlic, crushed
2.5 ml (½ tsp) salt

DRESSING
60 ml (4 tbsp) vegetable oil
30 ml (2 tbsp) white wine vinegar
10 ml (2 tsp) chopped fresh thyme
5 ml (1 tsp) Dijon mustard
Salt and ground black pepper

Mix the seasoning ingredients together in a bowl. Add the pork strips and toss. Refrigerate for 1 hour.

Boil the cubed pumpkin for about 7 minutes until tender. Drain and refresh in cold water. Place the dressing ingredients in a screw-topped jar and shake.

Cook the pork in four batches, using one-quarter of the oil for each batch of meat. Cook over a high heat, stirring frequently, for about 2 minutes. Set aside.

Place the sliced onion, green pepper, pumpkin and salad leaves in a bowl. Pour over the dressing and toss gently. Divide the salad between four plates and top each with one-quarter of the pork. Serve at once.
SERVES 4 AS A MAIN COURSE

RIGHT: Caribbean Pork Salad

ASIAN SQUID & SCALLOP SALAD

Vegetable oil for frying
8 large scallops
12 cleaned baby squid, about 275 g (10 oz) in weight
2 spring onions
1 starfruit
175 g (6 oz) Chinese cabbage
60 ml (4 tbsp) torn coriander leaves
Coriander sprigs, to garnish

LEMON GRASS DRESSING

1 small stalk lemon grass, very finely chopped
45 ml (3 tbsp) groundnut oil
25 ml (1½ tbsp) soy sauce
25 ml (1½ tbsp) lemon juice
10 ml (2 tsp) sesame oil
7.5 ml (1½ tsp) clear honey
1 large clove garlic, crushed

Place all the dressing ingredients in a screw-topped jar and shake well to combine. Set aside.

Lightly oil and preheat a griddle pan or heavy-based frying pan and cook the scallops over a high heat, for about 5 minutes on each side. Remove and set aside. Cook the squid in the frying pan for about 1 minute on each side.

Slice the spring onions on the diagonal and cut the starfruit into thin slices. Wash the Chinese cabbage and shred coarsely. Toss the coriander leaves with the cabbage and divide between four plates. Arrange the seafood on the plates with the spring onions and starfruit. Spoon dressing over each salad and serve at once.

SERVES 4 AS A MAIN COURSE

EXOTIC PRAWN & PINEAPPLE SALAD

175-g (6-oz) piece fresh pineapple
75 g (3 oz) cucumber
2 spring onions
75 g (3 oz) white cabbage
50 g (2 oz) Chinese cabbage
10 cooked king prawns, peeled but with tails intact
2 cooked king prawns, in the shell, to garnish
2 wedges fresh pineapple, to garnish
2.5 ml (½ tsp) sesame seeds, toasted, to garnish

DRESSING

25 ml (1½ tbsp) groundnut oil
25 ml (1½ tbsp) sesame oil
15 ml (1 tbsp) white wine vinegar
7.5 ml (1½ tsp) soy sauce
7.5 ml (1½ tsp) sesame seeds, toasted
5 ml (1 tsp) tamarind concentrate
5 ml (1 tsp) caster sugar

Place the dressing ingredients in a screw-topped jar and shake well to combine. Set aside.

Cut the piece of pineapple flesh into slim wedges. Peel and dice the cucumber and slice the spring onions on the diagonal.

Wash the two types of cabbage leaves and shred finely. Toss the shredded cabbage with half the dressing and divide between two plates. Arrange the pineapple, prawns, cucumber and spring onions on top and spoon over the remaining dressing.

Garnish each salad with a whole prawn and a wedge of pineapple. Sprinkle over the sesame seeds and serve at once.

SERVES 2 AS A MAIN COURSE

TOP: Exotic Prawn & Pineapple Salad
BOTTOM: Asian Squid & Scallop Salad

THAI BEEF SALAD

450 g (1 lb) beef fillet
275 g (10 oz) Chinese cabbage
175 g (6 oz) cucumber
175 g (6 oz) water chesnuts
1 fresh red chilli
1 small carrot
25 g (1 oz) coriander leaves
30 ml (2 tbsp) groundnut oil

MARINADE

2 stalks fresh lemon grass, finely chopped
5-cm (2-inch) piece root ginger, peeled and finely chopped
6 Kaffir lime leaves, finely chopped
2 shallots, finely chopped
4 cloves garlic, crushed
Juice of 2 limes
60 ml (4 tbsp) soft brown sugar
20 ml (4 tsp) tarmarind concentrate
10 ml (2 tsp) fish sauce (nam pla)
30 ml (2 tbsp) chilli oil

DRESSING

30 ml (2 tbsp) fish sauce (nam pla)
30 ml (2 tbsp) rice wine vinegar
30 ml (2 tbsp) groundnut oil
60 ml (4 tbsp) chopped fresh coriander
Pinch of sugar

Place the marinade ingredients in a large bowl and mix together. Slice the beef into long, thin strips and add to the marinade. Toss well and refrigerate for 1 hour.

Place the dressing ingredients in a screw-topped jar and shake well to combine. Set aside.

Shred the Chinese cabbage and cut the cucumber into long strips. Slice the water chestnuts and cut the chilli into rings. Peel the carrot and, using a canelle knife, make ridges along the length of the carrot;

then slice the carrot thinly to produce 'flowers'. Place vegetables in a large bowl with the coriander.

Heat a little of the oil in a heavy-based frying pan and fry the beef strips in batches over a high heat, stirring frequently until cooked – about 2 minutes.

To serve, pour the dressing over the raw salad and toss well. Divide between four plates and spoon one-quarter of the beef on each. Serve at once.

SERVES 4 AS A MAIN COURSE

THAI-STYLE PRAWN & PAWPAW SALAD

1 ripe pawpaw
450 g (1 lb) cooked, peeled prawns
100 g (4 oz) cucumber, cut into matchsticks
75 g (3 oz) beansprouts, washed
4 radishes, thinly sliced
175 g (6 oz) Webb's lettuce, washed and dried
Halved salted peanuts, to garnish

DRESSING

60 ml (4 tbsp) groundnut oil
30 ml (2 tbsp) sweet chilli sauce
10 ml (2 tsp) Thai fish sauce (nam pla)
2 small cloves garlic, crushed
1 small green chilli, seeded and finely chopped
Grated zest and juice of 1 lime
50 g (2 oz) salted peanuts, coarsely ground

Mix the dressing ingredients in a bowl and set aside.

Peel the pawpaw. Cut the fruit into quarters, re-move seeds and slice the flesh thickly. Place the prawns, cucumber, beansprouts, radishes and pawpaw in a bowl. Pour over the dressing and toss gently.

Divide the lettuce and prawn salad between four plates, garnish with peanuts and serve at once.

SERVES 4 AS A MAIN COURSE

RIGHT: Thai Beef Salad

MUNG BEAN & BASMATI RICE SALAD

2.5 ml (½ tsp) saffron strands
360 ml (12 fl oz) boiling water
100 g (4 oz) mung beans
100 g (4 oz) Basmati rice
30 ml (2 tbsp) vegetable oil
3 shallots, peeled and diced
100 g (4 oz) young leaf spinach, washed
2 large plum tomatoes, peeled, seeded and sliced
50 g (2 oz) raw cashew nuts
5 ml (1 tsp) sea salt

DRESSING

15 ml (1 tbsp) vegetable oil
15 ml (1 tbsp) lime juice
15 ml (1 tbsp) natural yoghurt
1 clove garlic, crushed
Sea salt and pinch of sugar

Place the safffron strands in a bowl with the boiling water and infuse for 30 minutes. Remove 15 ml (1 tbsp) of saffron liquid and add to the dressing ingredients in a large bowl. Whisk to combine and set aside.

Boil the mung beans for 30-35 minutes until they have begun to split. Drain and add to the dressing.

Place the infused saffron and its water in a saucepan with a little salt. Bring to the boil, add the rice and simmer for about 10 minutes until tender. Drain and add to the mung beans.

Heat 15 ml (1 tbsp) of the oil in a frying pan and sauté the shallots for 2 minutes over a medium-high heat. Add the spinach and sauté for a further minute. Transfer to the bowl of ingredients with the tomatoes.

Heat the remaining oil in a frying pan and fry the cashew nuts over a medium-low heat for 5 minutes, turning constantly until golden. Remove, drain on kitchen paper and sprinkle with sea salt. Add to the bowl. Toss well and serve at once. SERVES 4

ORIENTAL CRAB SALAD

225 g (8 oz) mangetout
225 g (8 oz) baby sweetcorn
100 g (4 oz) beansprouts
450 g (1 lb) fresh crabmeat, flaked
100 g (4 oz) young spinach leaves
Sliced fresh red chilli, to garnish

ROASTED CHILLI DRESSING

4 fresh chillies
15 ml (1 tbsp) grated fresh root ginger
120 ml (8 tbsp) sunflower oil
60 ml (4 tbsp) white wine vinegar
30 ml (2 tbsp) soy sauce
10 ml (2 tsp) soft brown sugar

Prepare the dressing. Place the chillies under a pre-heated hot grill and grill, turning once, for 3-4 minutes until skins are charred. Remove and allow to cool; then peel off skins, seed and chop the flesh. Place the grilled chilli flesh in a food processor with the remaining dressing ingredients and blend to produce a smooth dressing. Set aside.

Cut the mangetout in half and blanch in boiling, salted water for 30 seconds. Drain and refresh in cold water. Halve the sweetcorn lengthways and blanch in boiling, salted water for 1 minute. Drain and refresh in cold water. Wash the beansprouts. Place the crabmeat, mangetout, sweetcorn and beansprouts in a bowl. Pour over the dressing and toss gently.

Wash and dry the spinach and place in a shallow serving bowl. Spoon the crab salad into the centre, garnish with chilli and serve at once. SERVES 4

TOP: Mung Bean & Basmati Rice Salad
BOTTOM: Oriental Crab Salad

SALMON TERIYAKI SALAD

350 g (12 oz) salmon fillet, sliced into strips
15-cm × 2.5-cm (6-inch × 1-inch) piece kombu
seaweed, soaked in cold water for 2 hours
45 ml (3 tbsp) sesame oil
50 g (2 oz) mooli, peeled and cut into thin strips
50 g (2 oz) carrot, peeled and cut into thin strips
1 stick celery, sliced diagonally
2 spring onions, sliced diagonally
4 radishes, thinly sliced
50 g (2 oz) radicchio leaves

TERIYAKI MARINADE

45 ml (3 tbsp) shoyu soy sauce
45 ml (3 tbsp) mirin
15 ml (1 tbsp) caster sugar
15 ml (1 tbsp) sesame oil

DRESSING

30 ml (2 tbsp) sesame oil
30 ml (2 tbsp) rice wine vinegar
15 ml (1 tbsp) shoyu soy sauce
15 ml (1 tbsp) mirin
Pinch of caster sugar

Mix together the marinade ingredients. Add the salmon. Refrigerate for at least 1 hour. Place the dressing ingredients in a screw-topped jar and shake. Set aside.

Drain the soaked seaweed and cut into long strips. Heat 15 ml (1 tbsp) of the sesame oil in a frying pan and add the seaweed. Fry for 1 minute. Remove and cool. Transfer all the prepared vegetables to a bowl.

Heat half the remaining sesame oil in a frying pan and add half the marinated salmon. Cook over a high heat for 2 minutes. Remove and repeat.

Wash and dry the radicchio and divide between four plates. Pour the dressing over the prepared vegetables, toss and divide between the plates with the salmon strips. Serve at once.   SERVES 4

TOFU & ORIENTAL MUSHROOM SALAD

25 g (1 oz) dried shiitake mushrooms, soaked in
boiling water for 1 hour
50 g (2 oz) oyster mushrooms
40 g (1½ oz) flat field mushrooms
40 g (1½ oz) button mushrooms
25-g (1-oz) piece root ginger, peeled and shredded
30 ml (2 tbsp) vegetable oil
25 g (1 oz) butter
5 g (¼ oz) arame seaweed, soaked in cold water
for 2 hours
1 spring onion, cut into julienne strips
75 g (3 oz) Chinese cabbage, shredded
25 g (1 oz) carrot, peeled and sliced
15 g (½ oz) alfalfa sprouts
15 ml (1 tbsp) sesame seeds, toasted

DRESSING

100 g (4 oz) silken tofu
15 ml (1 tbsp) shoyu soy sauce
15 ml (1 tbsp) mirin
15 ml (1 tbsp) cider vinegar
10 ml (2 tsp) sesame oil
5 ml (½ tsp) soft dark brown sugar

Whisk the dressing ingredients and set aside.

Drain the soaked, dried mushrooms and cut in half. Slice the other mushrooms thickly. Place in a bowl and toss with the shredded ginger. Heat half the oil and butter in a frying pan and sauté half the mushrooms over a high heat for 2 minutes. Remove and repeat.

Drain the soaked seaweed and place in a large bowl with the cooked mushrooms, spring onion, Chinese cabbage, carrot, alfalfa sprouts and sesame seeds. Toss gently. Serve the salad at once with the dressing passed separately.   SERVES 2 AS A MAIN COURSE

RIGHT: Salmon Teriyaki Salad

GADOH GADOH

350 g (12 oz) potato, peeled and diced
100 g (4 oz) fine green beans, cut into
2.5-cm (1-inch) lengths
175 g (6 oz) fresh pineapple, cut into small chunks
100 g (4 oz) cucumber, diced
175 g (6 oz) mooli (white radish), peeled and cut
into thin matchsticks
100 g (4 oz) fresh beansprouts
100 g (4 oz) Chinese cabbage, finely shredded
50 g (2 oz) white cabbage, finely shredded
3 hard-boiled eggs, shelled and sliced
Prawn crackers
Coriander sprigs, to garnish

PEANUT SAUCE

1 stalk lemon grass, finely chopped
1 large clove garlic, chopped
2 shallots, chopped
1 large red chilli, seeded and chopped
1.25 ml (¼ tsp) shrimp paste
30 ml (2 tbsp) groundnut oil
100 g (4 oz) crunchy peanut butter
150 ml (¼ pint) coconut milk
Juice of 1 lime
10 ml (2 tsp) soft brown sugar
5 ml (1 tsp) dark soy sauce

Place the first five ingredients for the peanut sauce in a food processor and blend to a smooth paste. Heat the oil in a saucepan, add the paste and cook over a medium heat for about 5 minutes, stirring occasionally. Add the remaining sauce ingredients and cook, stirring, for a further 2-3 minutes. Set aside.

Boil the diced potato for about 8 minutes until tender. Drain and refresh in cold water. Blanch the green beans for 1 minute, drain and refresh in cold water. Place the potatoes, beans, pineapple, cucumber, mooli and beansprouts in a bowl and toss well.

Line a shallow serving dish with the shredded cabbages. Pile the tossed vegetables into the centre and spoon over the peanut sauce. Arrange the sliced egg and prawn crackers on top and garnish with coriander. Serve at once. SERVES 4-6

INDIAN SALAD

450 g (1 lb) potatoes, peeled and diced
100 g (4 oz) frozen peas
2 tomatoes
75 g (3 oz) onion, thinly sliced
432-g (15-oz) can chick-peas, drained

DRESSING

15 ml (1 tbsp) vegetable oil
5 ml (1 tsp) ground cumin
5 ml (1 tsp) chilli powder
10 ml (2 tsp) garam masala
60 ml (4 tbsp) mayonnaise
60 ml (4 tbsp) natural yoghurt
5 ml (1 tsp) lemon juice
60 ml (4 tbsp) mango chutney
Salt and ground black pepper

Prepare the dressing. Place the oil in a saucepan with the cumin, chilli and garam masala, and cook over a gentle heat for 1 minute. Allow to cool slightly, then mix in a bowl with the remaining dressing ingredients.

Boil the potatoes for about 8 minutes or until tender. Drain and refresh in cold water. Cook the peas according to the instructions on the packet. Plunge the tomatoes into boiling water to loosen their skins; when cooled, peel skins, seed and dice the flesh.

Place the vegetables and chick-peas in a bowl. Pour over the dressing and toss well. Allow to stand for 1 hour before serving. SERVES 4

RIGHT: Gadoh Gadoh

MOROCCAN LAMB & COUS-COUS SALAD

175 g (6 oz) cous-cous
30 ml (2 tbsp) olive oil
Salt and ground black pepper
150 g (5 oz) boneless, lean lamb, cubed
5 ml (1 tsp) ground cumin
2.5 ml (½ tsp) ground coriander
1.25 ml (¼ tsp) ground cinnamon
15 ml (1 tbsp) chopped fresh mint
50 g (2 oz) whole blanched almonds, toasted
50 g (2 oz) dried apricots, diced
½ red pepper, cored, seeded and diced
12 small black olives
30 ml (2 tbsp) snipped fresh chives
100 g (4 oz) Cos lettuce leaves, washed and dried
4 artichokes in oil, halved, to garnish

DRESSING

30 ml (2 tbsp) Greek-style yoghurt
45 ml (3 tbsp) olive oil
15 ml (1 tbsp) lemon juice
30 ml (2 tbsp) chopped fresh mint
1.25 ml (¼ tsp) ground cumin
Salt and ground black pepper

Place the cous-cous in a bowl and pour over boiling water to just cover. Set aside for 15 minutes. Fork the grains and stir in half the olive oil. Season well.

Place the lamb in a bowl and add the cumin, coriander, cinnamon and mint. Mix well to combine. Heat the remaining olive oil in a frying pan and cook the spiced lamb over a high heat for about 5 minutes, stirring until cooked through. Remove and add to the cous-cous along with the almonds, apricots, red pepper, olives, chives and seasoning.

Whisk the dressing ingredients in a bowl, pour over the salad and toss gently. Serve the salad on a bed of lettuce, garnished with artichokes.   SERVES 4-6

CURRIED TURKEY & BULGHUR WHEAT SALAD

225 g (8 oz) bulghur wheat
30 ml (2 tbsp) corn oil
2 small shallots, sliced
2 cloves garlic, crushed
30 ml (2 tbsp) mild curry paste
450 g (1 lb) turkey breast, sliced into strips
50 g (2 oz) raisins
100 g (4 oz) cucumber, peeled and diced
50 g (2 oz) Brazil nuts, roughly chopped
30 ml (2 tbsp) chopped fresh mint
30 ml (2 tbsp) chopped fresh flat-leaved parsley
30 ml (2 tbsp) lime juice
Salt and ground black pepper
Parsley and mint sprigs, to garnish

DRESSING

60 ml (4 tbsp) corn oil
30 ml (2 tbsp) white wine vinegar
10 ml (2 tsp) mild curry paste
Pinch of sugar
Salt and ground black pepper

Place the bulghur in a bowl and pour over boiling water to cover. Leave for 40 minutes until water is absorbed. Transfer to a clean linen and squeeze to remove excess moisture; place in a large bowl.

Heat the oil in a frying pan, add the shallots, garlic and curry paste and cook for 2 minutes. Stir in the turkey and cook for a further 5-6 minutes. Add to the bulghur wheat along with the raisins, cucumber, Brazil nuts, chopped herbs, lime juice and seasoning.

Shake the dressing ingredients in a screw-topped jar. Pour over the salad. Toss well to coat and serve at once, garnished with herb sprigs.   SERVES 4-6

TOP: Curried Turkey & Bulghur Wheat Salad
BOTTOM: Moroccan Lamb & Cous-cous Salad

FRUIT SALADS

Fruit salads make delicious desserts that are healthy and light, but you could also serve some of the recipes in this chapter for a brunch or breakfast. Included here are salad recipes appropriate for each season of the year, from the light and fruity Red Summer Berry Salad to the stronger flavours of Winter Fruit Salad, made with dried fruit, brandy and cinnamon.

STRAWBERRY SALAD WITH PEPPERCORN & ORANGE SYRUP

225 g (8 oz) caster sugar
360 ml (12 fl oz) fresh orange juice
Grated zest of 1 orange
10 ml (2 tsp) crushed pink peppercorns
5 ml (1 tsp) crushed black peppercorns
450 g (1 lb) strawberries

Place the sugar in a saucepan, add the orange juice and heat gently to dissolve the sugar. Bring the mixture to the boil and boil rapidly for 1-2 minutes until slightly syrupy. Remove from the heat and stir in the grated zest and crushed peppercorns.

Hull and halve the strawberries. Place the strawberries in a serving bowl and pour over the peppercorn syrup. Stir gently to mix, cover and chill for several hours before serving. SERVES 4

RED SUMMER BERRY SALAD

1 vanilla pod
700 g (1½ lb) red summer berries, such as strawberries, raspberries, redcurrants and tayberries
Strawberry leaves and flowers, to decorate
Macaroon biscuits and whipped cream, to serve

SUGAR SYRUP
100 g (4 oz) granulated sugar
300 ml (½ pint) water

Make the sugar syrup by placing the sugar and water in a saucepan and heating gently to dissolve the sugar. Then increase the heat and boil the syrup for 5-6 minutes. Cool and set aside.

Split the vanilla pod in half lengthways. Scrape out the soft centre and stir it into the sugar syrup. Discard the pod. Allow to infuse for 2 hours.

Prepare the berries, removing stalks and hulling as necessary, and place in a serving bowl. Strain the vanilla sugar syrup over the berries and stir in gently. Cover and chill in the refrigerator.

To serve, decorate the chilled salad with strawberry leaves and flowers, and serve with macaroons and cream. SERVES 4-6

TOP: Strawberry Salad
BOTTOM: Red Summer Berry Salad

PEACH, BLUEBERRY & CHERRY FRUIT SALAD WITH KIRSCH

2 ripe peaches
100 g (4 oz) cherries
175 g (6 oz) blueberries
Juice of 1 lemon
90 ml (6 tbsp) kirsch
25 g (1 oz) flaked almonds, toasted
Borage flowers, to decorate (optional)
Vanilla ice cream, to serve (optional)

SUGAR SYRUP
50 g (2 oz) granulated sugar
150 ml (¼ pint) water

Prepare the sugar syrup as instructed on page 64. Allow to cool.

Wash all the fruit. Halve and stone the peaches and slice them thickly. Halve the cherries and remove the stones. Place the peaches, cherries and blueberries in a serving bowl.

Stir the lemon juice and kirsch into the sugar syrup and pour over the prepared fruit. Stir gently, cover and chill thoroughly. Just before serving, sprinkle the toasted almonds over the fruit salad and decorate with borage flowers. Serve at once with vanilla ice cream, if desired.   SERVES 4

THREE-MELON SALAD WITH MUSCAT WINE & HONEY

Use a variety of melons of your choice for this fruit salad. The types suggested below make a colourful and delectable combination.

700 g (1½ lb) watermelon
450 g (1 lb) Charentais melon
450 g (1 lb) Galia melon
300 ml (½ pint) muscat wine
30 ml (2 tbsp) clear honey
Grated zest of 1 lemon
Fresh marigold petals, to decorate (optional)

Using a melon baller, make melon balls with the three different melons. Place the prepared melon balls in a large serving bowl.

Mix together the wine, honey and lemon zest and pour over the melon balls. Stir gently to mix, cover and chill the salad for several hours. Just before serving, scatter a few marigold petals over the salad.

SERVES 6

RIGHT: Peach, Blueberry & Cherry Fruit Salad

CARIBBEAN FRUIT SALAD

I large mango
½ medium pineapple
3 large oranges
2 large bananas
4 passion fruit
Grated zest and juice of 2 limes
90 ml (6 tbsp) coconut rum
Prepared Sugar Syrup (see page 64)
60 ml (4 tbsp) coconut flakes, lightly toasted

Peel the mango and cut the flesh from the stone. Slice the flesh and place in a serving bowl.

Peel the pineapple, remove the core and cut the fruit into chunks. Peel the oranges with a sharp knife, removing all the white pith, and cut between the membranes to produce segments. Add the pineapple and orange to the sliced mango.

Peel and slice the bananas and halve the passion fruit. Add the bananas to the bowl of fruit along with the pulp from the passion fruit.

Stir the lime juice and zest, and the rum, into the sugar syrup. Pour the syrup over the fruit, stir gently to mix and chill. Just before serving, sprinkle the coconut flakes over the fruit salad.   SERVES 6

TROPICAL FRUIT SALAD WITH LIME SYRUP

Prepared Sugar Syrup (see page 64)
Grated zest of 2 limes
Freshly squeezed juice of 3 limes
I small mango
I pawpaw
¼ medium pineapple
12 fresh rambutans or lychees
I starfruit
2 bananas
450 g (I lb) watermelon

Place the sugar syrup in a large serving bowl and stir in the lime zest and juice.

Peel the mango and cut the flesh into chunks. Peel and halve the pawpaw, remove seeds and slice the flesh. Peel and core the pineapple and slice the flesh. Peel the rambutans or lychees. Slice the starfruit and bananas and cut the watermelon into small chunks.

Add the prepared fruit to the lime syrup and stir gently to mix. Chill thoroughly before serving.

SERVES 6

TOP: Caribbean Fruit Salad
BOTTOM: Tropical Fruit Salad

RHUBARB, BANANA & APRICOT SALAD

450 g (1 lb) rhubarb
100 g (4 oz) caster sugar
150 ml (¼ pint) ginger wine
6 large, firm, ripe apricots, halved and stoned
30 ml (2 tbsp) finely chopped stem ginger in syrup
2 small bananas, sliced
Greek yoghurt or mascarpone cheese, to serve

Preheat the oven to 180°C (350°F, Gas mark 4). Wash the rhubarb and cut it diagonally into 2.5-cm (1-inch) lengths. Place in a shallow ovenproof dish and stir in the sugar and ginger wine. Cover the dish and bake the rhubarb for 20 minutes.

Remove the rhubarb from the oven, add the apricots to the dish and return to the oven for a further 15 minutes, until the rhubarb is soft but still holds its shape and the apricots are tender.

Using a slotted spoon, gently transfer the rhubarb and apricots to a serving dish and stir in the sliced bananas. Strain the syrup from the ovenproof dish into a jug, stir in the chopped stem ginger and pour over the fruit salad. Allow the salad to cool, then chill thoroughly before serving with yoghurt or mascarpone cheese. SERVES 4

LOW-CALORIE CITRUS FRUIT SALAD

3 pink grapefruit
2 yellow grapefruit
6 tangerines
6 kumquats
Honey or maple syrup
Fresh lemon balm, to decorate

Using a sharp knife, peel a grapefruit, removing all the white pith. Holding the grapefruit over a bowl, to catch the juices, cut between the membranes of the fruit to produce segments. Squeeze any excess juice from the fruit membranes into the bowl. Discard membranes and repeat with all the grapefruit.

Peel the tangerines with a sharp knife, removing all the white pith, and slice the fruit thickly. Wash and thinly slice the kumquats.

Place the grapefruit segments, tangerine and kumquat slices in a serving bowl. Strain the reserved fruit juice and sweeten with a little honey or maple syrup to taste. Pour the juice over the fruit and chill the salad. Serve decorated with fresh lemon balm.

SERVES 4-6

RIGHT: Rhubarb, Banana & Apricot Salad

GREEN FRUIT SALAD WITH MINT

15 g (½ oz) or a generous handful fresh mint leaves
Prepared Sugar Syrup (see page 64),
warmed slightly
30 ml (2 tbsp) freshly squeezed lemon juice
1 large green apple
225 g (8 oz) green-fleshed melon, such as Galia
4 kiwi fruit
100 g (4 oz) seedless green grapes
Mint sprigs, to decorate

Wash the mint and chop coarsely. Add to the warmed sugar syrup, stir well and leave to infuse for at least 2 hours. Then strain the syrup, discard the mint and stir in the lemon juice. Pour the syrup into a serving bowl.

Wash the apple, remove the core and slice thinly. Add the apple slices to the serving bowl with the mint sugar syrup.

Peel the melon and cut the flesh into small chunks. Peel and slice the kiwi fruit and wash the grapes. Add the prepared fruit to the serving bowl. Stir gently to mix, cover and chill the salad thoroughly. Just before serving, decorate the salad with fresh mint sprigs.

SERVES 4

WINTER FRUIT SALAD

350 g (12 oz) mixed dried fruit, such as prunes, apple rings, peaches, pears and apricots
50 g (2 oz) soft brown sugar
450 ml (¾ pint) milkless Earl Grey tea
1 long strip orange zest
1 cinnamon stick, broken in half
5 cloves
45 ml (3 tbsp) brandy
Mascarpone cheese or crème fraîche, to serve

Place all the ingredients for the fruit salad, except the brandy, in a saucepan. Bring to the boil, stirring occasionally. Reduce the heat, cover the pan and simmer the fruit gently for 20-25 minutes until tender. Stir the brandy into the salad. Serve the salad warm or chilled with mascarpone cheese or crème fraîche.

SERVES 4

TOP: Green Fruit Salad with Mint
BOTTOM: Winter Fruit Salad

SALAD DRESSINGS

Along with classic oil-and-vinegar-based dressings, such as the Italian Balsamic Dressing, this chapter features the creamy Blue Cheese Dressing and Guacamole Dressing, as well as unusual varieties, such as Watercress and Horseradish dressings. Use the lighter dressings for delicate leafy salads and the creamier alternatives for more hearty combination salads.

ITALIAN BALSAMIC DRESSING

90 ml (6 tbsp) extra virgin olive oil
30 ml (2 tbsp) balsamic vinegar
I clove garlic, crushed
I small shallot, finely chopped
Sea salt and ground black pepper

Place all the dressing ingredients in a screw-topped jar and shake to mix thoroughly. Taste and adjust season-ing, if necessary, and store in the refrigerator until re-quired. The dressing will keep well for several days and can be made in larger quantities for convenience.
SERVES 4

Variation: For a lighter dressing, use 45 ml (3 tbsp) olive oil and 45 ml (3 tbsp) sunflower or corn oil.

CLASSIC FRENCH DRESSING

90 ml (6 tbsp) extra virgin olive oil, preferably French
30 ml (2 tbsp) white wine vinegar
10 ml (2 tsp) Dijon mustard
2.5 ml (½ tsp) caster sugar
2 small cloves garlic, crushed
Sea salt and ground black pepper

Place all the dressing ingredients in a screw-topped jar and shake to mix thoroughly. Taste and adjust season-ing, if necessary, and store in the refrigerator until re-quired. The dressing will keep well for several days.
SERVES 4

CHIFFONADE DRESSING

90 ml (6 tbsp) extra virgin olive oil
30 ml (2 tbsp) red wine vinegar
5 ml (1 tsp) French dark mustard
2.5 ml (½ tsp) caster sugar
15 ml (1 tbsp) chopped fresh parsley
15 ml (1 tbsp) snipped fresh chives
30 ml (2 tbsp) finely chopped red pepper
I hard-boiled egg, shelled and finely chopped
Salt and ground black pepper

Place the oil, vinegar, mustard and sugar in a bowl and whisk well to combine. Stir in the chopped herbs, red pepper and hard-boiled egg. Season the dressing to taste and use as required. The dressing is best used as soon as it is made.
SERVES 6

TOP TO BOTTOM: Italian Balsamic Dressing, Chiffonade Dressing, Classic French Dressing

THOUSAND ISLAND DRESSING

60 ml (4 tbsp) vegetable oil
60 ml (4 tbsp) olive oil
60 ml (4 tbsp) mayonnaise
30 ml (2 tbsp) tomato ketchup
Juice of I orange
20 ml (4 tsp) lemon juice
20 ml (4 tsp) Worcestershire sauce
5 ml (I tsp) mustard powder
5 ml (I tsp) paprika
I small shallot, finely chopped
I large dill gherkin, finely chopped
30 ml (2 tbsp) chopped fresh parsley
Salt and ground black pepper

Place the first nine ingredients in a bowl and whisk well until thoroughly combined and smooth. Stir in the remaining ingredients. Taste and adjust seasoning, if necessary, and refrigerate until required.

SERVES 4-6

Variation: Substitute the tomato ketchup for 45 ml (3 tbsp) sun-dried tomato paste.

BLUE CHEESE DRESSING

175 g (6 oz) soft blue cheese, such as Fourme d'Ambert or blue Brie, stored at room temperature
45 ml (3 tbsp) soured cream
30 ml (2 tbsp) red wine vinegar
75 ml (5 tbsp) sunflower oil
30 ml (2 tbsp) water
25 ml (I½ tbsp) chopped fresh thyme
Pinch of sugar
Salt and ground black pepper

Place the blue cheese in a bowl and mash to a paste. Place all the remaining ingredients in a separate bowl

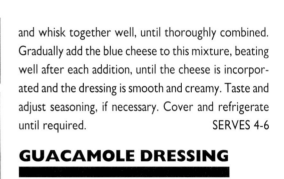

and whisk together well, until thoroughly combined. Gradually add the blue cheese to this mixture, beating well after each addition, until the cheese is incorporated and the dressing is smooth and creamy. Taste and adjust seasoning, if necessary. Cover and refrigerate until required.

SERVES 4-6

GUACAMOLE DRESSING

This dressing is excellent served with a simple crisp salad, as part of a Mexican meal.

I large, ripe avocado
Juice of 2 limes
60 ml (4 tbsp) olive oil
30 ml (2 tbsp) finely chopped red onion
½ large fresh red chilli, seeded and finely chopped
30 ml (2 tbsp) chopped fresh coriander
Salt and ground black pepper

Peel and stone the avocado and roughly chop the flesh. Place the avocado flesh in a food processor, add the lime juice and olive oil, and blend to produce a smooth paste. Season well and process again briefly.

Transfer the avocado mixture to a bowl and stir in the chopped onion, chilli and coriander. If the dressing is too thick, add a little water. Taste and adjust seasoning, if necessary. Cover and refrigerate the dressing until required.

SERVES 4

TOP TO BOTTOM: Thousand Island Dressing, Guacamole Dressing, Blue Cheese Dressing

PEAR & WALNUT VINAIGRETTE

This dressing is well-suited to salads that have blue or goat's cheese as one of their ingredients.

½ ripe pear
75 ml (5 tbsp) walnut oil
30 ml (2 tbsp) raspberry vinegar
Salt and ground black pepper
15 ml (1 tbsp) finely chopped walnuts

Peel and core the pear and roughly chop the flesh. Place in a food processor with the oil and vinegar. Process briefly to produce a smooth dressing.

Transfer to a bowl and season to taste with salt and ground black pepper. Stir in the chopped walnuts and use as required.   SERVES 6

HORSERADISH DRESSING

This dressing is ideal for beef salads and salads containing an oily fish, such as mackerel.

60 ml (4 tbsp) sunflower oil
60 ml (4 tbsp) cider vinegar
60 ml (4 tbsp) horseradish sauce
Salt and ground black pepper

Place the dressing ingredients in a bowl and whisk to combine. Taste and adjust seasoning, if necessary, and refrigerate until required.   SERVES 4

Variation: Add 15 ml (1 tbsp) very lightly whipped cream to produce a milder, creamy dressing.

WATERCRESS VINAIGRETTE

This vinaigrette combines well with fish salads and it is also excellent when used to dress a new potato salad.

50 g (2 oz) fresh watercress
2.5 ml (½ tsp) Dijon mustard
Salt and ground black pepper
150 ml (5 fl oz) extra virgin olive oil
45 ml (3 tbsp) balsamic vinegar

Wash and dry the watercress. Remove any large, tough stalks and place the watercress in a food processor with the mustard and seasoning. Process briefly to chop up the watercress.

Pour the olive oil in a thin steady stream into the food processor with the motor running to produce a thick, smooth dressing. Add the vinegar and process again briefly. Taste and adjust seasoning, if necessary, and refrigerate until required. This dressing will keep well for 2 days in the refrigerator.   SERVES 8

TOP TO BOTTOM: Watercress Vinaigrette, Horseradish Dressing, Pear & Walnut Vinaigrette

INDEX